penguin life

harmony

whitney hanson is the author of *home* and *climate*. through whitney's vulnerability and authenticity, she has connected with thousands of readers and adamantly believes that poetry is not a dead language; rather it is the key to unlocking true vulnerability, which leads to deeper connection with one another. whitney grew up in rural montana, and she now lives in south carolina.

harmony

whitney hanson

life

PENGUIN BOOKS
An imprint of Penguin Random House LLC
penguinrandomhouse.com

A Penguin Life Book

LIBRARY OF CONGRESS CATALOGING-IN-PUBLICATION DATA
Names: Hanson, Whitney, author.
Title: Harmony / Whitney Hanson.
Other titles: Harmony (Compilation)
Description: 1st edition. | New York : Penguin Books,
an imprint of Penguin
Random House LLC, [2023]
Identifiers: LCCN 2023017150 | ISBN 9780143138013
(paperback) | ISBN 9780593512104 (ebook)
Subjects: LCGFT: Poetry.
Classification: LCC PS3608.A72336 H37 2023 |
DDC 811/.6—dc23/eng/20230413
LC record available at https://lccn.loc.gov/2023017150

Printed in the United States of America
3rd Printing

Set in Adobe Caslon with Didot Italic and Guadalupe Essential
Designed by Sabrina Bowers

for anyone who has outlived
someone they love

though i am often in the depths of misery, there is
still calmness, pure harmony and music inside me.

—VINCENT VAN GOGH

contents

introduction

there are never enough words.

whenever i complete a book i always feel it is a bit unfinished. it is a challenge to squeeze all my feelings and experiences into the binding. the story in these poems was more challenging to tell than any other i have explored. no matter how many poems i completed, no matter how much i revised and rearranged, i still felt like i couldn't do it justice.

eventually, i had to accept that the story was never going to feel finished. when i think about it now, it seems appropriate that i should feel so unsatisfied with a book written about grief. there is nothing more inconclusive than the feeling after you lose someone you love. there is nothing easy about misplacing a piece of yourself.

so, this is my message to you. i hope that in these pages you find a friend. i hope that you feel a little less lonely. i hope you find some peace. but if you reach the end, and your heart is still a bit broken, know that it is normal to feel that there are never enough words.

melody noun

mel·o·dy

a rhythmic succession of single tones organized as an aesthetic whole

a single note echoed out into the universe
you
at the very beginning of your story
loud and unafraid

now imagine your entire life
each moment a single note in the song
each rise and fall in the music
each breath between notes
each element of the beauty

this is your melody
a string of notes
dancing along the pages of your life
the composition of you

you begin with hope. the kind that is unwavering, untouched by the hands of heartache. please, clasp that hope between your palms as tightly as you can. as if you are a child and there are fireflies trying to escape your fingers. and when it becomes dark, because it will, peer between your pointer finger and your thumb and remember that there is light.

little one,

don't ever let the word sensitive be used as a weapon against you. keep your heart soft and spirit gentle. it is a gift to break even for the moth in the spider's web or the bird with broken wings.

a three-word question

who are you?

it is so easy for me.
i simply list everything i love
from the stars
to the sun
to the feeling of the wind in my hair
when i run

it is simple
i am everything i love
and that is enough

it is summer. i am 10 years old, running through sprinklers in my backyard, and my biggest concern is how cold the water feels when it hits my sun-kissed skin.

little one,

you built a sandcastle on the beach
you didn't worry about the tide washing it away

i envy you a bit
what is it like to create so carelessly?
what is it like to assume everything will stay?
what is it like not to worry that a change in the tide might
take everything you love away?

the snow is not snow
it is an opportunity to build a fortress

the grass is not grass
it is an opportunity to run barefoot

the clouds are not clouds
they are an opportunity to imagine

the river is not a river
it is an opportunity to swim

the music is not music
it is an opportunity to dance

you are awake but you pretend to be asleep so someone will pick you up and carry you to bed. you sink into the warm blankets, your favorite nightlight casting a soft glow on your head. this is how the end of the day is meant to feel.

soft and gentle and safe.

on windy days
i spread my arms
and close my eyes
and if i concentrate hard enough
i begin to fly

catch the leaves in autumn
go outside when it rains
watch thunderstorms at night
build blanket forts
pick wildflowers
admire rocks and seashells on the beach

collect all the simple treasures
the world has to give

little one,

love is simple for you
i'm sorry that i call you naive

i don't think you're naive
i think i'm jealous

you are far better at love
than i could ever be

notice the sounds of a busy house
music in the kitchen
tv in the living room
the sound of your sibling's laughter
spilling out the open door in the hall
soak it all up
because one day
you'll be on your own
wondering where
the laughter
disappeared to

they say when you grow up in a burning house you think the whole world is on fire.

i didn't grow up in a burning house. i grew up in a house where we hid the fire. i grew up in a house where everyone was secretly burning on the inside, but we didn't dare speak of it. i grew up in a house where we wore our armor like a badge of honor and pretended that nothing ever hurt us. for so long i thought it was only me who felt like i was deteriorating from the inside.

now i put my flames on paper. because i need you to know that there are others whose fires are kept inside like a scorching secret.

i will not let you burn alone.

my favorite trees to climb
are the weeping willows
they are the only ones
i feel truly understand me

to the souls born into this world
with a somber nature

to the people who are more like rain clouds
than rays of sunshine

to the children
of the weeping willows

they only reject you because they fear you
they only fear you
because you make them
feel something

your rain clouds are not your weakness
they are your superpower

i am passionately blue

i'm so lonely
not like i'm missing someone who left
more like i miss
a part of me i've never had

duet: a composition for two performers

i lived in the dark

not figuratively

i lived miles and miles from the city in a place where you

almost feel you could touch the stars if your reach your hand

up

what a wonderful beginning

the stars were my first best friend

you were my second best friend
i think you rivaled the stars

meeting you
was like putting
the last puzzle piece
in place

you will meet people who pull you
the way the ocean pulls the tide
you will find hearts
that feel cozy next to yours
as if you've known them your whole life
embrace this feeling
whether it is a lover or a friend
hold on to those hearts
hold tight to those hands

somewhere at the beginning of time
i think that your heart was a part of mine.
two souls fallen from the same star
found two different people far apart.
all my life i've looked for you
and all of yours you've been searching too.
today we met for a second-first time
but on ground instead of the sky.
i didn't know it
i couldn't see
that meeting you
was meeting the missing part of me.
~platonic soul mates

i like being alone
but that is why i knew you were different
because for the first time ever
i wanted someone else's company
more than my own

we are lying, shoulders pressed into a trampoline, counting the airplanes as they fly by. i'm wishing i could freeze this moment. stop the world from turning, keep the sky forever blue, and stay right here with you.

we draw a venn diagram on a crumpled piece of notebook paper. we list everything that makes us different and everything that we have in common. i think it's beautiful that we find little pieces of ourselves in other people.

i'm in love with the space
where our hearts overlap

in the half-awake hours
when everything becomes a bit sillier
and secrets become a bit easier to tell

we stay awake giggling
until the sun begins to rise
we sneak out barefoot into the grass
to meet the starry night
it is during these hours
that i know
what it means
to feel alive

i have always loved the way
music could make the world feel
like it doesn't exist
as if suddenly all my fears
are swept away

who knew
that there are people out there
who could make me feel the same way

we sit in the trees
in a small town
where the streetlights glow yellow

we sit in the trees
and laugh until the branches
drop leaves

we sit in the trees
and we learn more about happiness
than anyone on the ground

when your home is full of anger, and brokenness, and slamming doors

you can build a home here in my heart. one where you talk and i listen. one where you're safe to laugh as loud as you want or cry if you need to. one where every feeling you experience you can express fully.

i want you exactly as you are.

what a privilege it is
to have someone
i can be so fragile with
~true friend

when i tell you that you are the sun to me
i don't mean the sun in mid-july
when everything feels warm
and you have to squint your eyes

i mean the sun in the dead of winter
when i haven't seen the clouds part in weeks
when i've felt cold for so long
that i can't recall how it feels to be warm

suddenly you arrive
from behind my overcast sky
and remind me
what it is to feel light

so when i say that you are the sun to me
i don't mean to sound cliché
it's just that before you
my skies were always gray

where are all the love poems written for the friends who were more loyal than any lover ever was?

usually, you don't recognize these moments when they are happening then suddenly you look back and realize how important it was that your mom tucked you in at night or how comforting it was to hold the hand of your first best friend. it isn't until years later that you begin to miss the nickname that your dad called you at 8.

when i write about you
i feel guilty
as if i am plagiarizing
the most exquisite piece of art
trying to repaint a masterpiece
with lines and dots on paper
forgive me
for attempting to replicate
the universe i see in your soul

we have built the kind of friendship, the kind of love, that is indestructible. you tell me the worst you've done, and i will tell you that i love you. i show you the darkest rooms in my heart and you build a fire and ask to stay the night.

"do you think you'll forget me someday when we are grown, and we live in different states?" she asked.

"i don't think so," i said.

but this is what i should have said.

"i will remember you every time someone makes me laugh or each time someone gives me a space to share a secret that has been burning in my chest. i will remember you when anyone picks up the phone at an inconvenient time or whenever someone holds me when i cry. how does one forget a person who taught me so much about friendship? to forget you would be to forget how to love."

i never have to ask
when it begins to rain
i just go outside
and know that you will do the same

we are like brothers and sisters
the people of the rain
you have my heart
if you come alive on stormy days

tell me why they left you
i will tell you why i stay
tell me that you made a mistake
i will tell you it's okay
tell me you're sorry
i will tell you there is nothing to apologize for
tell me who you are
i will tell you that you are more
tell me your heart is broken
i'll tell you i feel it too
tell me you hate yourself
i will tell you i love you
~what friends are for

"how do you know she is your person?"

"because when i want to run away,
she is who i'm running toward."

dear peter pan,

i leave my window
open every night
in case you ever
want to fly inside

the before:

the before is a time of simplicity. it is a period of light, innocence, and music. it is dancing without a care and loving without restraint. the before is beautiful but do not become lost here. there will be an after and there will be love there too.

trust me.

i once met a girl who was like wildflowers
lovely but never here for too long

i loved her more
than the gardens of perennials
that seem to never die

little one,

i usually don't like to issue warnings to my younger self, but i would like to tell you this. i exist, i live on the other side of what you're about to face. and i find joy here. i find hope here. i still cry sometimes too. the sorrow you will meet is going to make you feel like someone silenced all the music in the world. i will not downplay the soul-wrenching, darkness-conjuring power of grief.

but i will tell you this,
i am still here.
you will survive the night.

rest noun

rest

a silence in music

you took the
music with you
when you left

on your last day on earth
i went to eat breakfast at 1 a.m.
it had been an entire day since i had eaten anything,
or maybe it had been a week.
i couldn't recall. but either way, i wasn't hungry.

when there is one specific thing that you want with your entire
being, there is no room for food or water or anything else. all i
wanted at 1 a.m. was to see you walk through the door but all
i got were pancakes and eggs.

the morning after you
lose someone you love
the morning after you
cry yourself to sleep
the morning after you
realize your life will never be the same
~heartbreak hangover

the first time i ever received flowers for a gift
wasn't from a person trying to win my heart
or as a congratulations for graduation
or some other special accomplishment

no, the first time i received flowers
it was accompanied by a condolence card
as if tulips would ever patch
my broken heart

i ran the dishwasher fifteen times today
just to drown out the silence eating my brain

old death looks like autumn
but young death looks like snow in the spring

old death is anticipated
part of the natural way of things
but young death looks like
wilted leaves
that had just begun to grow
frozen flowers
under a foot of snow
saying goodbye
just after you said hello

gone is not a concept i am good at comprehending. i know *here*. *here* is easy. *here* is your hand in my hand. *here* is my head in between your collarbone and chin. *here* is you humming the same song that i always pretend drives me crazy.

but *gone*. *gone* doesn't make sense. *gone* is like trying to draw pictures of the wind. *gone* is blank stares at ceilings and blank pages filled with tears. i can't understand my empty hands. i can't find a place to rest my head. and i can't fathom that you'll never drive me crazy again.

receiving sympathy
is not capitalizing
on your grief

the funniest (not so funny) thing about all this is that you were the one with all the goals and the plans. you knew exactly what you wanted your future to look like. but me, i've been stumbling along, tripping over the word purpose for years.

now you're gone
and i'm still here

how unfair.

i wish i had someone to blame

i don't talk about it
because when i say it out loud
when i squeeze it into a measly sentence
it seems so small and insignificant
but inside of me
these feelings are
the entire sea

this is not a metaphor
i am broken
i am a million pieces on the floor
i am in a storm begging the sky for mercy

and this is not a metaphor
i am the darkest part of the ocean
the coldest part of the depths
every hope i ever held is washing out to sea

and this is not a metaphor
i am a tragedy
i am the crushing feeling of a final goodbye
the tears sting so much i think
i am bleeding from my eyes

and this is not a metaphor
i am everything and nothing all at once
grasping at straws and gasping for air
hoping in the next breath you will be there

and this is not a metaphor
i am trying to become anything
so that you will be mine and i will be yours
but none of this is real

and this is just a metaphor

you drew all the curtains
and closed all the blinds
you crawled in bed
and turned off the lights
you forgot what it was like
out there with the sun

you didn't want to feel light
when inside you there was none

i write frantically, obsessively to recall every detail of your life. i document each memory. i try so desperately to keep you, but somehow i always find myself disappointed. words cannot capture the way your laugh sounds or the feeling of your fingers laced in mine. lines and dots on notebook pages cannot replicate the sunshine in your soul or the warmth that pours from your eyes. i know that no amount of paper and ink will bring you back. still irrationally and relentlessly i try. without reward, without restraint, without reason i write.

sometimes i think that death made a mistake
that he was out searching for someone else to take and maybe
you were just caught in his path. maybe you weren't meant to
leave so soon. maybe you were just in the wrong place.

did you know that at its deepest point the ocean is 35,876 feet deep? for some perspective, that is the same distance that airplanes fly above the earth. the same distance that it takes to shrink trees and houses down to specks on a landscape.

in the ocean, at that depth, there is little life and absolutely no light. the pressure of the water is crushing to anything with a spine.

that's the only way i can describe those first few weeks after you left. it was as if water and darkness filled every space inside me. i was small and becoming smaller by the minute.

i was disappearing
and i was okay with it.

what do i do with all that is left over?

your tote bag of clothes is still in the corner of my room where you left it the last time you spent the night. i can't bring myself to move it. moving it would be like admitting something. it would be like surrendering to reality.

my heart can't do that yet.

i have this reoccurring dream where you come back, like you were just on a long vacation. you walk back in the door with suitcase in hand and everything is just as it was.

then i wake up.

i don't think there has been a time
when i was in greater necessity of a god
or greater uncertainty that there is one

i wrote a letter for you to open
on your 16th birthday
i never imagined i would
read that letter to you
from your bedside in a hospital
before you ever turned 16

i'm awake at 3 a.m. again and i can't help but remember a time when i would stay up until this hour just to talk with you.

i'm awake at 3 a.m. again and i think i can hear our laughter trapped in the walls even though nothing seems funny to me now

i'm awake at 3 a.m. again but everything is different this time because you only exist inside my head.

imagination is cruel at 3 a.m.

i can't hold back the sea

i feel that if anyone holds me
it might give my heart
permission to fall to pieces
so i distance myself
in an attempt to remain whole

some days
i take sledgehammers to the walls
i pull out fistfuls of hair
i yell curses at the sky
i clench my fist until my nails
create crescent-shaped marks
on the palm of my hands

some days i miss her
as violently as i can

some days
i cry without making a sound
i plead with the stars
i draw mascara stripes on my face
i heap myself into
a hopeless pile on my bed
i tuck all my anger away
and replace it with sadness instead

somedays i miss her
as quietly as i can

today i framed all the pictures
we took together
then i hid them
in the back of my closet

today i read all the notes
you left me
then i shoved them
into a box under my bed

one moment i am
frantically trying to remember you
the next i am
hopelessly trying to hide my pain away

my body is betraying me today
i tell it to move
and it stays
i ask it to rise
and it crumples to the floor
i beg it to go on
it tells me i can't anymore

fight or flight

this is supposed to be
the body's reaction to trauma
but me
i am frozen
i can't run
i can't fight
i can't move

this morning i woke up to a world that you weren't in and i was certain all the flowers should have died, but outside the sun is shining and the tulips are poking their heads through the soil.

i can't help but think how disrespectful it is that the sunflowers have the audacity to grow.

will i ever be able to forgive myself
for living when you're not here?

i think it breaks
the moon's heart too
when she looks down to see
me without you

grief causes the kind of tiredness
that sleep cannot fix
~your eyes rest but your heart does not

i don't think there is anything pretty about the kind of sobs that rack your chest when you experience loss this deeply. i refuse to romanticize the incredible pressure in your rib cage or the way it feels like your heart is collapsing in on itself. i will not deceive you into believing that your pain is anything but wretched and devastating and real.

remember that time we played hide-and-seek. i counted to one hundred then opened my eyes. after twenty minutes i couldn't find you anywhere. after forty i began to get nervous. when i finally found you, i was in tears. i was certain i might never find you.

it feels a little bit like that now. like a silly game of hide-and-seek. at first i was sure i would find you soon. after a few weeks the true meaning of the word gone sunk in. now it's been months. i know you're not going to appear, but this little part of me keeps hoping the game might end.

it's not your fault
it's not your fault
it's not your fault

i'm suffocating
under the weight of
the words i didn't say
and the love i didn't give
~regret

91.95 million miles
the distance between the earth and the sun
but the sun rises every day and i see her
the sun sets every night and i say goodbye

6 feet
the distance between your heart and mine
but somehow it feels farther than
the distance between the earth and the sun

91.95 million miles
and i watch the sunset every night

6 feet
and i never really got the chance to say goodbye

i used to have nightmares
that i could only escape
when i was awake

now i live in a nightmare
that i can only escape
when i'm asleep
~avoidance

maybe i don't want perspective

yes, three years from now
this won't matter so much to me
but right now
this is everything
right now
i am ruined

slow down
slow down your thoughts for just a moment
slow down your worries
slow down your heart

i know that you have a tendency
to feel nothing at all
until you feel everything at once
and everything at once
feels like it's too much right now
but you can handle this
this overwhelming feeling is going to pass
like every other storm has before
the waves are going to go from 10 feet tall
to tiny ripples on the shore
feel the air fill your lungs
take one breath
and take one more

tie your heart back down to your chest
and your feet back down to the floor

i remember the way you used to make me laugh through my tears. you always knew how to fix it when my heart was falling apart. but now my heart is in pieces. i don't know where you are and i don't know where to start.

i can't decide if time
is my enemy
or my friend

time takes the pain away
but time takes you away too

i have anchored myself to grief
i have become my loss
it is the only way
i know how to keep you

i'm afraid that
i'm becoming a person
you wouldn't recognize
i'm afraid your ghost will
come to find me tomorrow night
and when you discover
this empty shell i've become,
you'll simply pass me by
searching for the girl you used to love

it is impossible to unlace
my heartstrings from yours
how do i untangle
a connection authored by the stars?

the scariest part
is that i feel like
i'm starting to unknow you

how cruel of the world
to take you from me
twice

i read all the messages i sent you
in the weeks after you died
i started to feel guilty
that it has been months since i sent one

i know that you're the one who left
but forgetting makes me feel like
i'm abandoning you

lift the weight from your shoulders
allow me to hold it for you
and after you turn the page
let some of your heaviness
become wedged between these pages

perhaps my broken heart
can keep yours company

i stare into the darkness at the place next to me and if i try
hard enough, i swear i see you sleeping there.

~*mirage*

every time i lose someone new
it isn't just one loss
it is every loss i've ever felt.
~grief is cumulative

i'm in a room full of people
who used to call you a friend
and it's like no one else notices
everyone is going about their day
laughing and talking and living

i have this resentment
boiling up in my chest
how can they just forget
that you're not here?

recently i learned
that resentment isn't a function of anger
it is a function of jealousy

perhaps
i'm not angry that they are living without you
i'm jealous that i'm not

my heart has been feeling claustrophobic in my rib cage. i can hear it planning its escape in the night. i can feel it tugging at my insides in the day.

i've become so lost
my heart doesn't even feel
at home.

you blinked
and suddenly it was all taken away from you
that feeling of security
ripped from beneath your feet
you cannot blame yourself
for feeling so uneasy
you cannot shame yourself
for shaking as you try to stand again
it is okay if battles that used to be easy
seem to take everything within you to win

is getting older just a series of funerals?

i want to just give up on everything
but the laundry is piling up
and dinner isn't going to make itself
so, i gather up the dirty clothes
while i wonder if i'll ever feel whole again
i boil a pot of water while i contemplate how it might feel to
just disappear
i wonder if everyone else feels the same way
and i hope they don't
but secretly hope they do
because at least then i wouldn't feel so alone
the only thing worse than everyone understanding my
darkness
is no one understanding at all

on the days when the darkness weighs you down, repeat this
phrase

just one more day
just one more day you rise
just one more day you wipe tears from your eyes
just one more day you make yourself breakfast
just one more day you shower
just one more day you brush your hair
just one more day you go on

just one more day
you will survive

if you are gone
but you are still part of me
what does that make me?

half?

i'm watching from the rooftops
as cars go by
and life moves forward without me

~stuck

they all said it
"she's mature for her age"

what they meant
is that i didn't tear the town apart
when i lost you
i simply swallowed it all and went on

"she's mature for her age"

they liked to use that as an excuse
to forget that i was so young

my heart is rotting in my chest
and you do nothing
but complain of the smell

how i felt:

i am so deeply unwell that i don't know how to say it in a way
that you will understand.

what i said:

i'm fine.

i get so sick of the *going to*

it's *going to* get better
life is *going to* be good again
you aren't always *going to* feel this way

i know that one day it will be better
but what do i do with this shattered heart today?

the kind of anger that accompanies grief is different than any other kind of anger. it is anger with no object. fire with nothing to burn. so it catches on to every person around you that doesn't deserve to be burned.

friends

lovers

god

yourself

death is a villain
that doesn't ever take one victim at a time

today
i'm holding a funeral
for the part of me that died with you
the part of me that loved easily
and viewed the world through innocent eyes

i am picking flowers for the ceremony
decorating the walls of my heart
hanging pictures of the girl that was me
but isn't anymore

i am mourning myself
crying over the gravestone of memories
that used to belong to *us*
but belong only to *me* now

death is a villain
that doesn't ever take one victim at a time

when they buried your heart in the dirt
they also buried mine

i am fully submerged in water
and everyone keeps asking
if i need any help

can't they see
i can't speak underwater
i can't even breathe

i am in seattle for the first time

whenever i go somewhere new
i feel a little sad
that you didn't get to see it too

ten

nine

eight

its new year's eve and i can't stop thinking of every holiday
like a monument, a tally mark on the chalkboard of special
moments i will be spending without you.

seven

six

five

they count down the seconds to a new year while i scratch
one more mark signifying the end of my first full year i've
spent without you.

four

three

two

one.

on the worst days
i don't miss you

to miss you is painful
but not missing you
means i'm forgetting you
and that
is much
much
worse

i don't want your sunshine and roses
and i don't want to keep my composure

i want to throw glass plates on the floor
i want to shatter the fine china
i want to slam all the doors
i want to scream at the clouds and stomp on the ground
i want to take sledgehammers to the rafters
i want to bring the sky down
i want to set fire to the gardens
i want to burn every rose

i'm so sick and tired of staying composed

i didn't talk about it
i stored all my anger in my bones
and slowly lost all my friends
because of how bitter i became
~side effects

all i know of anger is shame

why can't i just scream
without worrying what
someone might think?

little one,

you've been so strong but it's been so long and the waves just keep coming. one after another they leave you gasping for air, swimming to the surface just to be swallowed by the next disaster. i know you're tired in every way a person can be tired. but please keep fighting. i promise, the waves won't always crash like today. i promise, your heart won't always feel this way.

sometimes i feel so out of place in this body. i look in the mirror and flinch at how grown up the girl staring back at me is. i think part of me is frozen in the moment you left. part of me is still sitting in the trees waiting for you to meet me here. a piece of me is still staring at my phone waiting for you to call. growing up and changing is like a testament to how far away you really are now.

you feel so close
but oh so far
i feel so big
but oh so small

little one,

i'm sorry
you had to
grow up this way

remember when we tied blankets
around our neck
and ran around the house like superheroes
we felt so indestructible
i wonder

who is going to save me now?

when you cannot find the strength
to stay for yourself

stay for the sunset you are meant to see three years from now

stay for the stranger crying in a bathroom stall that you will
comfort on a random wednesday in june

stay for the keys you will find on the ground and the relief on
the face of the owner when you return them

stay for the chocolate milkshake you will order when your
friend orders vanilla so you both can have a taste of each

stay for that song you will introduce to a friend that will keep
them alive on their darkest nights

you don't always see
all the light you give to the world
but i do
and i hope you stay

sometimes you try your hardest
you do all the right things
you drink your water
you exercise
you go outside
but something inside of you
still feels dark
~there isn't a formula for healing

if the tide rises
let it carry you.
if the sun rises
hold her hand too.

if you don't have the strength
to rise to your feet
let yourself be held
by the sun and the sea.

i'm not trying to hurt people
but there's a war inside my brain
so whenever someone gets too close
they intercept some of my pain
~*i'm sorry*

i'm afraid i'm the girl that your mother warned you about. the kind who is a little too damaged to love. the kind that you can tell will break your heart before you've gotten the chance to learn her middle name. i am the result of too many closed doors, too many goodbyes, too many tattoos for people who have died. i am nothing if not self-aware but being aware of my tendency to run away from love doesn't make me any less likely to panic the instant you try to get close. i won't stand in your way, but one day you will find out that i'm the girl your mother warned you about.

there is this numbness
that exists inside me
in the place
where love used to live

i'm lying on your chest
and i can hear your heartbeat
i think some people
find that sound comforting
but to me it sounds like
a clock
a metronome
always counting down
reminding me of how fragile
it all is

i am in a dark, silent room
and the door is locked
i have the key
but i pretend i don't
because i don't really want to leave
~self-inflicted misery

dear peter pan,

i'm not sure i believe in neverland anymore
but sometimes late at night
i open my window
and i'm certain
that if i jumped
i could fly away

when your entire existence feels dark and there is no music left inside you, remember that a rest is not the end of a song. it is merely a pause in the music. a moment to remember how beautiful the last part of the melody was. i know it feels like you are drowning. but believe me, you will breathe again. you will live again.

crescendo noun

cre·scen·do

a gradual increase in the volume of music

the music is beginning
to filter back into my bloodstream
at first, muffled and somber
but slowly
surely
i'm beginning to remember how it felt
when my heart thumped along
to the melody inside me
some days it is upbeat and happy
most days it is quiet and sad
but regardless
the sound is slowly coming back

i believe that there are two kinds of grief.

the first develops immediately after loss. it is the type that tears at your soul and twists you into knots that you don't think will ever unravel. it is the sinking feeling of loved ones in hospital beds and people whose hands you'll never hold again.

the second is the string of yarn once you've untangled it all. it follows you. it snags on shadows that look like the silhouette of people you once loved. it catches on the corner of your smile and reminds you that love is a temporary gift.

at the end of the day, it is this second kind of grief that saves us because it ensures we never forget how precious it all is.

i know
more than anyone
that nothing i can say
will mend the hole in your heart
so first
forgive me for trying

i will proudly claim
you are the best thing
that has ever happened to me
no matter how it ended

i heard a song today
that i knew you would love
but you're gone
so instead i got in my car
and sang it as loud as i could
and hoped that somewhere out there
you heard me

that is precisely it

you don't know
you don't know when it will feel okay again
you don't know where this life is headed
you don't know if tomorrow
will be your best day or your worst
you don't know how to get rid
of the ghosts that haunt you at 3 a.m.
you don't know and maybe that's the point

maybe there is hope in the mystery

"why are you so sad all the time?"

"life feels safer this way. you can't take anything from empty hands."

just the thought
of entering a hospital again
makes it difficult to breathe
~*flashbacks*

you may never have closure and
it might not work out in the end.

in the end you will wonder why. you will likely be tortured
with questions for the rest of your life. you learn a lot about
grief and a tiny bit about acceptance. eventually it may become
easier to live with this sadness. your unanswered questions
might become more comfortable to carry. but i will not
promise you that every wound you have will heal completely.
some scars we carry for our entire lives.

to grieve is not a unique experience and i am not special. i know that this is the way of the world. everyone aches for someone who is gone. everyone carries shadows that they keep hidden under their smile. but i can't fathom how everyone else keeps their sadness so politely.

sometimes i want to set the world on fire.

i hope someday you decide that it is time. time to open the doors and pull the curtains aside. time to let in the light and roll up the blinds. i hope someday you feel ready for life to be bright. but i will be patient with you.

~all in your own time

i break in unexpected places now. i don't always know why but sometimes at a bus stop on a random wednesday in january i notice how empty the world feels without you.

it is so inextricably human
to feel
exactly the way you do
right now

i've been afraid of stillness
for a long time
when i quiet everything else
when i calm my busy life

you are the only thought
that occupies my mind

things i'd like to tell you about:

i got the tattoo we were supposed to get together. it was strange walking into the tattoo parlor alone.

i found love, then lost it again, then found it. i'm learning that's just how love goes.

i turned 17 then 18 and suddenly i'm 22. i don't feel much wiser and i can't believe you've been gone for this long.

i took 7 airplane flights this year. airplanes are my favorite place to miss you. you seem a bit closer when i'm in the sky.

i hear that song
i close my eyes
and in every way
i am with you
~music has memory

i still know our secret handshake

i worry
that someday i won't cry anymore
when i look at pictures of you

i'm trying to accept
that tears are not the only evidence
that i miss you

how dare i waste a single breath
when you didn't waste one
and you were given less

the heart is a muscle
and like all muscles
it has memory
the unconscious ability
to repeat what it knows

my heart knows you
it knows the pattern of your breathing
and the sound of your laughter
it knows the way your sock-covered feet
sound on tile in the morning

my heart knows the look on your face
when you're concentrating
it knows the strain in your eyes
and the twitch of your nostrils
when you're trying to hold back tears
it knows you as if it has known you
for a thousand years

and although i know my heart would continue to learn you
until the end of time
my heart knows that occasionally
forever becomes redefined
by fate or mortality or poor timing
forever falls apart sometimes

so if mortality takes you
if fate is unkind
if forever falls apart
there are a million neurological pathways
that spell your name in my heart

i miss the way the stars looked
reflected in your eyes
i have never seen a more worthy mirror
for infinity than you

i don't have dreams
about you coming back anymore.

does that mean i have healed
or does that mean i have run out of hope?

it has been so long
that no one understands why

but i still cry
on the fourth of july

they call it letting go but truthfully, it's nothing like letting go. you don't get to dangle your heartbreak over a cliff and then release it when you feel like you're ready. you don't suddenly get to drop your pain into a void and never speak to it again.

instead you learn to carry your hurt more comfortably. you sew pockets in your soul that you can tuck your grief away in. and little by little it gets easier to hold it all.

some days i decrescendo
i sink back into my sadness
these days heal me
just as much as the days the music is loud
the silence is necessary
just as much as the sound

you have been taught
not to engage with your pain
to push it down where no one sees

you don't have to hide here

i'm particularly talented
at breaking my own heart

over
and over
and over again

it's okay
fall to pieces
scream into your pillow
let yourself break

but this time
when you're done
when you find the strength to stand
let the heartache stay on the floor

i pray that you never gain the wisdom that causes your hands
to shake when your loved ones take a little extra time to
answer text messages

but if you do
and delayed texts
make it difficult to breathe

you're not alone

perhaps life
is just a process
of collapsing
being reborn

when i tell you it's going to turn out okay i don't mean that one day everything that is wrong will be put right, i don't mean that every expectation you have will be met, i don't mean that there will be no more bad days.

i mean that the sun has set on every bad day you've had before. i mean that the world will continue to turn. you will breathe and begin to learn that sometimes being okay means that this isn't where your story ends.

tomorrow we begin again.

you loved fully
lost everything
and survived

don't you dare believe
you are anything but resilient

you had to dig up the soil
and peel back layers of your skin
just to feel the warmth of the sun again

do not bury yourself again
so carelessly
do not dishonor your battle
by crawling back to the ground

it is not inherently human to reject help.
it is learned. somewhere you convinced yourself that you
must do this all on your own.

this is a lie.

how frequently i fluctuate
between none of this matters
and it all matters
far too much

to the critic.

isn't it a strange task to place a rating on another
person's grief or on another human's method of escaping the
dark places in their mind? tell me, what does it require to
receive a five-star rating on the obliteration of my heart? what
is the correct way to fall apart on paper? what is the proper
way to spell out *my* story?

when you're grieving people always like to tell you to take as long as you need. it's okay to feel your pain for as much time as you need to. but i think it is important for you to hear this too.

it is okay to stop grieving. it is okay if it doesn't hurt anymore. you don't have to feel guilty for not being in pain. your healing does not invalidate how deep your wound once was.

your growth does not erase your love.

grief will teach you one of two lessons

how to run from love
or how to run toward it

you choose which lesson you learn

when you have a good day, even if you don't come by them often, pick up something as a reminder. a tiny rock or a wildflower, a penny you find on the ground. place it on your windowsill. then when the darkness returns you will have something real to remind you that there is good.

you've made a lot of promises to other people
to stay by their side
to look out for them
to have their back

when will you start looking out for
the girl on the swing set
the girl singing at the top of her lungs
the girl with dreams bigger than the sky

when will you take care of her first?

i always hug people
as if i am trying to absorb them
into my bloodstream
and maybe that is my problem
because i can't love you
without trying to make you part of me

i have a hoarding problem

i save every little note
the gum wrapper you folded into a heart
the receipt you scribbled lopsided stars on
every tiny piece of love
anyone has ever given me
i cling to it
like it might disintegrate
if i look away

i collect rocks. i keep them in a dish on my bathroom
counter. i need to hold on to something that isn't going to
expire before me.

i crave permanence.

"i'll be here in the morning"

that's what you tell me every night
before i sleep
and i can't help but imagine
how it's going to ruin me
if i ever wake up
and you aren't there

your fear of abandonment is entirely justified

nothing in this world stays forever
the leaves eventually fall
the fields of sunflowers wilt
even the best people
leave sometimes

you're not crazy
you're observant

little one,

how long has it been
since anyone has held you,
like really held you?

one day
out of the blue
i began to run again
with arms out like airplane wings
i closed my eyes
and before i knew it
i started to fly

how i've missed myself

sometimes i wonder if atlas was never really holding up the sky, he just believed that he was, and that belief was crushing enough.

today i cry
for the wilted daisies
while i plant the seeds
for tomorrow's flowers

you are stronger than the ocean
mightier than the waves
when life stole your music
you chose to stay

dear peter pan,

i'm not sure how you missed my letters but suddenly i'm 22 years old and i'm not so certain i'm interested in talking to you anymore. i do however have just one request.

when i was 16 my best friend left for neverland and never came back. i know this may never reach her or you or anyone at all. but if this message in a bottle washes up on your shore, can you tell her i'm still here, but my heart is a little torn.

do you hear that?

that beat in your chest like a drum. that hum of life like a
symphony within you. even the way you breathe is music. you
are coming back to life. reuniting with yourself.

oh what a magnificent sound.

you are clenching your fists
until you draw blood from your palms
from holding on for so long

don't you know
it hurts less
to let it all go
than it does to keep holding on?

harmony noun

har·mo·ny

the combination of simultaneous musical notes to create a beautiful sound

i am finally finding a balance,
a great harmony
between the loss
and the love
between who i was
and who i have become

i grew up with the understanding that good experiences were a reward and bad experiences were a punishment. so you can imagine that when my best friend died, i felt like it was some sort of judgment upon me. i scrutinized myself in pursuit of the moment i went wrong. i carried the weight of her fate on my shoulders like a well-kept secret.

i have come to know that sometimes terrible tragedies happen to good people. without explanation or justification. i have finally stopped blaming myself for circumstances that were so out of my control.

now, this is what i need you to know. your experiences are not a reflection of your character. you are good, light, and kind. you are not deserving of all the darkness you have experienced or the injustice you have seen. nothing you have done has warranted this cruelty. sometimes this world is just mean.

there is no such thing as love that is wasted.

every late-night phone call
every laugh until we cry
every inside joke
every meet me between your house and mine
every pizza at 2 a.m.
every dance party in your room
every secret handshake
every piece of me and you

this love is forever ours
even though you left too soon

i look up at the clouds and see your heart floating by
i gaze at the sea to find the color in your eyes
i catch your scent in the breeze
your legs swinging from the trees
and even though you seem so far
i promise to never stop finding you
in the clouds
and the trees
and the stars

you are allowed release the ache in your chest
without erasing the love you had
~*give yourself permission to heal*

i see the pain in your eyes
and grief uncurls her fist
and offers me the only kindness
she has to give
~empathy

and of all the songs that play in my heart
ours will forever be my favorite

it is our human tendency to think of life in terms of story arcs. the protagonist goes on a journey of self-discovery, then she endures the greatest of trials, finally she overcomes them, and the story ends.

in life, the story doesn't end. you turn the page and you are left with this giant question.

what now?

who are you if you're not
at war with something?

who are you when you're living
not just trying to survive?

the healing is just as inevitable as the heartbreak. one day, without warning, you get out of bed without having to battle the sadness weighing you down. one day you find yourself dancing without hesitation, smiling easier, laughing harder. one day, without trying, you feel alive.

stop exchanging your life
for your misery
stop paying your time
into the pockets of the past
~live today

i'm painting the walls white today.

they were already white, but time and life has turned them a dirty sort of gray. so, i'm painting over them. starting over. puttying over the holes and covering up the scuff marks around the floorboards.

your heart is tattooed with scars
etched with the names of people
who are constellations now

i think it is beautiful
that you hold the night sky
in your chest

it's okay
to miss the child you used to be

it's also okay
to miss the child you never got to be

the reality is that nothing is yours to keep forever. so you borrow time, love, and joy. you check them out like books from a library and you try not to spend your life mourning moments in time or missing people who were never yours to keep.

instead you cherish each page you turn. you stain some with tears and you are filled with joy on others. when it is over, you place the books back on the shelf. and you cry for the end of the story while you pick up the next book.

this is how you begin again.

i'm standing in the rain
and the water is filling my boots
and i don't care
for once i am drowning
in something other
than my sadness

today
i starve my misery
today
i give my sadness nothing to eat
today
i will not let grief consume me

when you begin loving
the world around you
you will suddenly find
it loves you back

the words
i love you
never used to get
stuck in my throat
~*hesitation*

it doesn't come easily to you anymore, *loving*.

it is a constant war in your head between your fear and the child inside who blew kisses into the wind. you might not like it, but this is how you will have to love now. you will have to blow kisses into the wind regardless of the fear. you may not be able to love with ease, but you will be able to do something even greater.

you will learn to love with courage. you will learn to love despite all the loss you have felt, despite how many times your heart has felt shattered, despite the loves you've outlived.

i believe that love before loss is a special gift but i think there is something even more incredible about a love that takes courage to give.

it may be difficult to imagine
but you will find love
that feels steady and healing
instead of anxious and uneasy

the day you let love in again. allow yourself to fall hard. crash recklessly into the arms of a lover or a friend. the day you decide to love again do not enter the doors with hesitation. throw open the gates of your heart. smash through the cloudy window glass and let the light consume you like a flood.

there is this emphasis we place on the search for romantic love while we disregard platonic love entirely. stop embarking on noble quests to find your soul mate and please just go get coffee with your friends.

you are not returning to yourself
this is not a journey that comes full circle where you once
again become the person who has never been hurt

you will never be that person again

you are not returning
you are reuniting
with a piece of yourself
that you lost
you are inviting the person you were
to be a part of who you have become

i look at strangers on the street
and i don't want
to talk to them about the weather
and i don't want
to hear about how busy
the bank was this morning

i want to know if they've ever been so broken that they
cannot cry quietly
i want to know if they
visit ghosts at night too
i want to know who they were five years ago
and how they've changed
and why they've changed
and who they've left behind

i don't care about the weather
let me see your bones

they will tell you that love is free
but it's not
that is the beauty of it
it will always be
a risk to love
but it will always be
a risk worth taking

you do not belong to your grief
do not let it drag you
to every dark corner it finds

you are the master of your heart
carry yourself gently back into the light

things you should do more often:

share your feelings,
go on walks,
listen,
say i love you,
give without the expectation of return,
ask your grandparents to tell you
stories of their life,
smile at strangers,
appreciate the little things,
have deep conversations,
compliment others on their personality
not just their appearance,
spend more time outside,
look at the sky,
forgive,
write letters,
laugh,
hug,
read poetry

dissonance:

in music it is the tension or clash resulting from the combination of two disharmonious notes.

in life it is the grief that plays in the background of love. it is the uneasy pinch in your gut when you remember all there is to lose.

i think i've always loved autumn
because it reminds me
that even as nature crumbles
as the leaves fall
and the grass loses its pigment
there remains something enlivening
about watching the world around
succumb to a peaceful death
it is comforting to be reminded
that decay
is in the nature of being
so in my crumbling
in my death and decay
it is humbling to be reminded
i am no greater
than the grass or the trees
i rise and i fall
and that is the way of things

if you ever get the chance to love a person who knows grief,
do not let them go.
you see, the thing about grief
is that it's not exclusive
it consumes life
it taints everything a little gray.
it won't hesitate to remind you
that everyone and everything you love
will disappear someday.
but i've found that the people who carry grief
love with a fierceness that no one else knows.
they understand what's at stake
because they've had to let someone go.
so they remember the little things
and they show up when it counts
they know that life is rare
you won't have to spell it out.
so don't take for granted
the people who know loss
for they know more about love
because they know what it costs.

healing requires visiting versions of your past self and treating them with kindness.

i had never seen someone treat the fire
with such contempt
as if the very substance of the sun
was beneath her
i watched her step through flames
without a flinch and
in an instant i knew
only a being who had
always lived in the destruction of flames
could ever look pain
directly in the face
as if it was only an inconvenience to her

i am certain
that before she would ever fear the fire
it would fear her first

there is no individual person or moment in your life that is *the destination*. there are simply slices of light along the way and people who feel like sunshine rays.
~*thank you for being my temporary sunshine*

you must be tired of learning lessons. you've been told how much you can grow from the darkness and adversity, but you're exhausted from being taught by your pain.

today, you take notes from the light. today you are learning how to be still without guilt and how to grow without shame. there is much to learn from grief. but oh what a relief to be a student of the sun.

they tell me "it all happens for a reason"

and i gently cover the ears of the child within me then
whisper to her.

"you did not deserve this
and this is not your fault"

little one,

with glistening eyes
and fists colored white
i'm here to stay
you don't have to hold on so tight

i remember standing by her
when i was only three feet tall.

i love
how she still
makes me feel so small
~the ocean

someone asked me that three-word question today,

"who are you?"

for a moment i hesitated, unsure

then from within me spilled
the stars and the sun
and the feeling of wind in my hair when i run
i poured out kitten paw prints
and pieces of art that make me cry
i pulled from my pockets the feeling of cozy blankets and
snowflakes dancing in the sky
i emptied everything i loved from my heart
and handed it over triumphantly

once again i am sure
i am everything i love
and that is enough

not many people will tell you this

you wear your sadness
just as elegantly
as you wear your joy

you wear your tiredness
just as gracefully
as you wear your strength

you wear your defeat
just as boldly
as you wear your victory

i am going to live
in this moment fully
in case i am never met
with another quite like this

"tell me your secret"

i ask the small child within

"how do you find hope"

she stoops down, picks a dandelion, and blows seeds into the wind. then she smiles and says,

"make a wish"

grief knocked on the door today
but i am not home

i am in the meadow
making friends with the wildflowers
and singing to the breeze

most people are so scared they won't even admit they are afraid. but your ability to speak how you feel doesn't make you weak, it makes you brave.

~*vulnerability*

i accidentally stepped on a flower
i sang to it as it died
and i thanked it for reminding me
how temporary it all is

you are the kind of person who questions whether the
darkness is lonely. you stay up past sunset just to ensure that
there is someone to comfort the night.

i admire the way
you find space in your heart
even for the dark.

it is the moment
you surrender to the waves
it is the instant
you allow the current to sweep you away
it is only when you stop fighting

that you realize you don't need to swim
you could float all this time

today i asked the trees to teach me about photosynthesis. i begged them to show me how to be filled with light. they invited me to sit in the branches and collect sunlight with the leaves.

it's been far too long
since i've spent the day in the trees

take off your shoes and walk barefoot in the grass. allow the earth to remind you that the best things in life are simple and require little to experience them.

sit with your feet planted in the dirt and learn to be attentive to the way the ground is steady and never fails to hold you even when everything else seems chaotic around you.

lay with your shoulder blades planted in the earth and remember how small all of this is. allow your worries to melt into the clouds.

simple is enough

i do not ask the sunrise
to be anything more
why should i expect
so much of myself?

insignificant
that is always the word that comes to mind
when i stare up at the sky

it's strange how insignificance doesn't bring me fear or
despair anymore
it gives me peace

how wonderful it is
the sky doesn't depend on me

today we went to the pumpkin patch
i asked you the most important question there is to ask

do you like your pumpkins tall and skinny
or do you like them short and fat?

we laughed at the funny-shaped gourds
we got lost in the corn maze
we stopped thinking about life
i think that was one of my favorite days
that i've had in a very long time

you asked me to describe love in one word
and i told you it was the ocean
you asked me why
and i told you that it is
one of the only things
that terrifies me
yet i wouldn't hesitate
to let it consume me

do you hear that?

the sky is calling your name
the sun is longing to touch your skin
the stars have been whispering
about your absence

all you have to do
is step outside

i do not want to speak incessantly about my pain.
i want to rant and rave about the way the flowers look covered
in morning light. i want to ramble relentlessly about the color
of the sky. if i obsess over something, please don't let it be my
heartache. let it be how breakfast tastes or the scent of the
rain.

when your world becomes light, do not neglect the person
you used to be. i hope you harbor no hate for the girl crying
silently in her bed.

she was only doing the best she could
with the cards in her hand.

i hope some days that little voice inside you fights back when you speak all the ugly words about yourself.

you are not cold
you are not empty
you are not dirty
you are not broken

you are still the girl
with soft heart
and wonder in her eyes.

just so you know it can be that simple again.

you can climb trees if you want to. you can ride bikes and fall asleep in the passenger seat on the way home. you can catch fireflies and you can sing and dance and wear silly clothes. you can put mac and cheese on the prongs of your fork and you can jump in the leaves. you can roll down hills and learn to walk on your hands. you can build blanket forts and you can pull all-nighters with your friends. you can cry and laugh and sleep under the stars.

and you can love without reason or hesitation
without expectation or condition or fear.

please allow yourself to live while you're here.

did you know that
it's free to go outside
and look up at the sky?

to all the children secretly burning inside:

what if one day we let it out
what if we opened the doors of our rib cages
and stopped trying to stifle the emotions
and cover the flames
what if we became recklessly honest
and excruciatingly real
what if we showed them
how we really feel?

we would set the world on fire

i am here

as long as your
fingers can turn the pages
as long as it takes
for paper to crumble to dust
i am here hidden in this book
waiting for you to come back
any time you need to be reminded
that you are loved

suddenly i am not afraid anymore
i'm looking up into the vastness of the sky
and i can feel the music fill all the spaces
that have been empty for so long

how wonderful it feels
to be alive

i cannot wait for the beautiful life you are going to live. i cannot wait for the day you move into your first home and dance around in the empty kitchen in your socks. i can't wait for you to take naps under clean sheets with a dog at the foot of your bed. i can't wait for you to sip tea in the evening while you watch the sky turn orange. i can't wait for you to wake up in the morning and realize.

you have such a beautiful life left to live.

dear peter pan,

i think i'm okay
right here where i am

acknowledgments

i cannot thank you enough for the opportunity you have given me to share my heart with you. so first, thank you for picking up this book. i love watching a book transform from *my* story into *ours*.

thank you to the team at penguin life who helped this book come together. a special thank-you to Meg Leder, Ruth Bladen, Emma McNamara, and Laura Lee Mattingly. you have brought this book to life.

Home

but if you can find a home within yourself
and make peace with your bees
you will be alright
—from Home

Resonant, raw, and vibrant, *Home* is a lyrical map to navigating heartbreak. Tracing the stages of healing, from the despair that comes with the end of a relationship to the eventual light and liberation that come with time, the poems in *Home* provide comfort and solace, while revitalizing your soul—and helping you make peace with your bees.

PENGUIN BOOKS